GW00481825

Some of the handwriting rules and 'choices' you should have remembered.

<u>Rules</u>:

Try to keep all your straight downstrokes parallel. Remember that all similar letters are the same height. Spaces between words are the size of the small letter 'o'.

<u>Choices</u>:

You may write f or f, s or s, d or d, d is better only at the end of a word.
You may join t from the bottom, or the cross bar; to ti tr tl th tk.
You may join e as in bee, eve, reed.
You may join o, r, v, w these ways,
— on rn vn wn, and oh rh vh wh.

Some letter patterns.

hshshshshshshshshshshshshshshshs

arararararararararararararararara

dldldldldldldldldldldldldldldld

rmrmrmrmrmrmrmrmrmrmrmrm

ohohohohohohohohohohohohoho

cdcdcdcdcdcdcdcdcdcdcdcacd

lmlmlmlmlmlmlmlmlmlmlm

veveveveveveveveveveveveveve

dududududududududududud

aoaoaoaoaoaoaoaoaoaoaoaoa

miniminiminiminiminiminim

sususususususususususususu

fofofofofofofofofofofofofofofofof

wowowowowowowowowowowow

unununununununununununu

wvwvwvwvwvwvwvwvwvwvwr

ohohohohohohohohohohohohoh

springsummerautumn

revereverevereverevere

You may
use
patterns,
letters or
words, or
groups of
words.

Practise this symmetrical layout.

Here lies
in a horizontal position
the outside case of
THOMAS HINDE
Clock and Watchmaker
Who departed this life wound up
in hope of being taken in hand
by his Maker and being
thoroughly cleaned, repaired &
set a-going in the world to come.
On the 15th of August 1836
In the 19th year of his
life.

from *A Small Book of Grave Humour*
Edited by Fritz Spiegl

A passage to copy.

"What would you like to eat ? Name anything. Think of your favourite meal and name it."

Peter thought. "Fried sausages and mashed potatoes with plenty of tomato sauce ; a cup of tea with three teaspoons of sugar and some ice-cream."

"Right!" said Greyfur. She thrust a hand into her pouch and pulled out a chair and table. She dipped again and out came a tablecloth, then knives, forks & spoons, pepper and salt, and a bottle of tomato sauce. Finally, with a flourish and a bow came the sausages and ice-cream.

from *Whispering in the Wind* by Alan Marshall

Copy these, them make up some more.

As wet as a fish - as dry as a bone;

As live as a bird - as dead as a stone;

As plump as a partridge - as poor as a rat;

As strong as a horse - as weak as a cat;

As hard as a flint - as soft as a mole;

As white as a lily - as black as coal;

As hot as an oven - as cold as a frog;

As gay as a lark - as sick as a dog.

ROAST CAMEL'S HUMP

A recipe from the *New Larousse Gastronomique* - cookery book

Bosse de Chameau Rôtie.

Only the hump of a very young camel is prepared in this way.

Marinate with oil, lemon juice, salt, pepper and spices. Roast in the oven as for beef.

When the crust is formed, the heat must be lowered. Baste frequently with the fat which will be floating in the dripping pan. Serve with its own gravy, and watercress.

The ideal school for me would be
Made of glass and suspended in a tree.
You swing on a grapevine
   from door to door
And classes would never be a bore.
Parachuting from a tree
   would be the main activity.
The tree in which the
   school would stand
Would hold the great
   big loyal school band.

Wynn-Anne Cole.

I dance on your paper,
I hide in your pen,
  I make in your inkstand
My little black den;
  And when you're not looking
I hop on your nose,
  And leave on your forehead
The marks of my toes.
  I drink blotting paper,
Eat penwiper pie,
  You never can catch me,
You never need try!
  I leap any distance
I use any ink
  I'm onto your fingers
Before you can wink.

ing ial our ough ness ure ied ed

ing ial our ough ness ure ied ed

ight tion ley ine ent age ive ove

ight tion ley ine ent age ive ove

ish ous well ick rds ham ttle ies

ish ous well ick rds ham ttle ies

ote ise oon ice ige able ound les

ote ise oon ice ige able ound les

ing ial our ough ness ure ied ed

ing ial our ough ness ure ied ed

ight tion ley ine ent age ive ove

ight tion ley ine ent age ive ove

ish ous well ick rds ham ttle ies

ish ous well ick rds ham ttle ies

ote ise oon ice ige able ound les

ote ise oon ice ige able ound les

Face the situation fearlessly, and
soon there will be no situation to face.

Anon.

An irritable man is like a hedgehog rolled
up the wrong way, tormenting him -
self with his own prickles.

Thomas Hood.

When love and skill work together
expect a masterpiece.

Ruskin.

The man who makes no mistakes does
not usually make anything.

E. J. Phelps.

Children aren't happy with nothing to ignore,
And that's what parents were created for.

Ogden Nash.

Here are some new alphabet sentences to try.

About sixty codfish eggs will make a quarter pound of very fizzy jelly.

Quick blowing zephyrs vex daft Jim.

Kegs of exquisite fuzzy plants will rejuvenate blighted compost.

Zippy hovercraft jockey along beside quays except midweek.

Joe was pleased with our gift of quail, mink, zebra, and clever oryx.

Alfredo must bring very exciting news to the plaza quickly.

The king and queen wisely decided to re-open the box, when out jumped a very fuzzy cat.

Very quickly a herd of prancing zebra ran away from the exhausted jackal.

The crimson kite zig-zagged twixt the jade-green sea, blue sky and flint-paved quay.

and a Latin sentence from Spain written in 1565
Gaza frequens libycum duxit Karthago triumphum.

from
The Law of the Jungle
by Rudyard Kipling

Now this is the law of the jungle
    as old and as true as the sky;
And the wolf that shall keep it
    may prosper,
But the wolf that shall break it
    must die.
Ye may kill for yourselves, and your
    mates,
And your cubs as they need & ye can;
But kill not for pleasure of killing,
And seven times never kill man.

A Riddle.

My first is in house
But not in mouse.
My second's in open
And round as can be.
My third's in run
And also in race.
My fourth's in hiss
And sounds like it too.
My last is in see
And rhymes with tree.
My whole if you pass
Is in a field full of grass.

Tim's watching came to an abrupt end. After so long in the tree, almost three hours, his foot developed cramp. He moved it to ease the discomfort and dislodged a piece of bark which fell in a shower of pine needles. The badgers disappeared down the hole in a skidding flurry of sand. Tim knew he would see no more of them that night.

But he did not mind. If ever an evening had been well spent, it was this one.

from *Bryn of Brockle Hangar* by Glyn Frewer

If a young chimpanzee is put into a room with an ordinary chair, for example, it starts out by investig- ating the object, tapping it, hitting it, biting it, sniffing it and clambering over it. After a while these rather random activities give way to a more structured pattern of activity. It may, for instance, start jumping over the chair, using it as a piece of gymnastic equipment. It has 'invented' a vaulting box, and 'created' a new gymnastic activity.

from *The Human Zoo* by Desmond Morris

HERALDRY

bend   chevron

Heraldry records the histories of old families. Because shields were important to knights, their achievements of arms were displayed on them.

The signs and symbols used on shields are called CHARGES.

The bend and the chevron above are two of them. The special colours used are called TINCTURES.

ARGENT - silver; OR - gold;
AZURE - blue ; GULES - red;
SABLE - black; VERT - green.

pale

pall

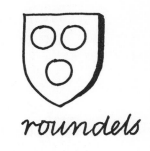
roundels

QUARTERING: When two families married, their coats of arms were combined. Their different kinds of CHARGES would be put into various quarters of the new shield Charges can be objects or animals.

HERALDIC ANIMALS may be drawn
with forelegs raised – RAMPANT
sitting – RAMPANT SEJANT
walking – PASSANT
lying down – COUCHANT
leaping – SALIENT

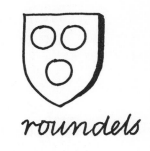
rampant

From a letter written on papyrus by a young
Greek boy to his father about 2000 years ago.

Theon to his father Theon,
greeting:
It was a fine thing of you not to
take me with you to Alexandria.
I won't write a letter or speak to
you, or say goodbye to you, and
if you go to Alexandria I won't
take your hand, or ever greet
you again. That is what will
happen if you won't take me......
Send me a lyre, I implore you;
if you don't, I won't eat, I won't
drink. There now!

10th March 1957

Darling Meg,

This is the way to write :-
Take a pot of ink and a pen —
either a goose or turkey quill or,
failing them, a wooden pen-holder
with a metal nib. Hold it so that
your fingers are at least 3/4 inch
from the point.... Do not wipe the
nib in your hair or on your face.
Do not suck it. You will find that
you remain perfectly clean.

If you balance a basket of eggs
on your head while writing it
will help cure the curvature of
your spine.

A passage to copy.

"And what about your men Robin?"
I said. The old outlaw looked at the
floor. "It's a question of pride, I suppose.
We were strong then. We knew what
we were fighting for. All that's
gone. I see Will Scarlet in the
Post Office, now and again. We pass
the time of day."
    "And Friar Tuck?"
"He went religious again. He's in a
monastery in Scotland."
    "And Marion?"
Robin lifted that bald head, and
there was sunlight in his face.
    "Oh she's still with me Jim. No
trouble there. We like the.....quiet life."

The dinosaurs are not all dead
I saw one raise its iron head
To watch me walking down the road
Beyond our house today.
Its jaws were dripping with a load
Of earth and grass that it had cropped.
It must have heard me where I stopped,
Snorted white steam my way,
And stretched its long neck out to see,
And chewed & grinned quite amiably.

Charles Malam

Some Tongue - Twisters.

When a twister twisting would twist him a twist,

For twisting a twist three twists he will twist;

But if one of the twists untwists from the twist,

The twist untwisting untwists the twist.

A proper crop of poppies
   is a proper poppy crop:
A proper cup of coffee
   is a copper coffee cup.

A passage to copy.

"It's like dreaming," whispered Jonathan, floating, his eyes shut. "Let's hold hands."
Hand in hand they floated gently together over the brow of the next hill, their feet just brushing the tops of the tallest grasses, their shadows trailing long and slanting behind them. Larks rose twittering and shrilling their surprise from underneath & a flock of crows high above cawed and croaked their amazement to see the humans drift so easily with the wind.
"Keep away, keep away, there's enchantment about, watch out,' they warned each other.........."

from *The Wishing People* by Nina Beachcroft

"Good night then: sleep to gather strength for the morning. For the morning will come. Brightly will it shine on the brave and true, kindly upon all who suffer for the cause, glorious upon the tombs of heroes. Thus will shine the dawn. Vive la France! Long live also the forward march of the common people in all the lands towards their just and true inheritance, and towards the broader and fuller age."

Winston Churchill
from a broadcast to the French people
October 21st 1940

Some advice from a 16th century writing master.

To set your letters even, above and belowe,
Maketh your writing the better to showe.
Between each letter keep equal distance,
That one with another have no resistance.
Your whites & yr blacks observe with good heed,
Which maketh yr writing more seemly to read.
Between word & word keep one letters space,
Leave nothing undone, that giveth a grace.
Keepe uniformitie from first to the last,
And alwaies beware you write not too fast:
For writing fast, before you write the better,
Will cause at last, you make not one good letter.
With scantling alike, let each word be plaste:
By keeping these rules yr writing is graste.
   from,
'The Writing Schoolemaster'
by Peter Bales   1590

The Principles of Good Writing

No matter what so-called style of writing we practise, in Western countries the principles are the same. Our modern handwriting is based upon a joined form of the Roman alphabet. This has been so for over 1,000 years.

The historic shape of our writing has developed for reasons of legibility and speed. It consists of ovals and straight lines parallel in pattern,

oioiololoioiololoioiololoioiololoioiol

Good writing also has a slight slope to the right, that is, in the direction of movement.

Practising The Letter Shapes.

It is most helpful when practising the letter shapes, always to practise writing them in their family groups.

e.g.

r n m h p b k , c o a g d q e , v w x i u y t l . etc.

Do <u>not</u> practise in rows of one letter like this,

a a a a a a a a a a a a a a

as although it may be useful as a pattern, this will not help your eyes and muscles to learn the important relationships in letters

How many letters here ? þ m g .

Flourished capitals.
Use these for the beginnings of paragraphs,
letters and titles occasionally. Don't overdo it!

A B C D E F G H I J

K L M N O P Q R S

T U V W X Y Z

The Principles of
Flourishing.

A P I L Q

Dear Rosemary,
A Happy Birthday.
Every Good Wish,
Yours Sincerely,
George

The Probable Origins of Some Words To Do With Writing.

Album - from albumen, eggwhite, painted on wooden writing boards

Book - Anglo-Saxon bóc, a beech tree, tablets of beech bark were written on.

Library - Latin, liber the inner bark of a tree, used to write on.

Paper - Papyrus, an Egyptian reed from which paper was made.

Pen - Penna, Latin for a feather.

Quill - Old English, quylle, a reed, and Latin calamus, a reed.

Style - Stylus, Latin for a Roman pointed bone for scratching wax.

Volume - Latin, volumen, a scroll.

Remember............

There are Three Levels of Handwriting.

First : Formal Writing; this is for
careful display work, signs,
maps, invitations, applications
for jobs and so on.

Second : Informal Writing; this is
for everyday school work,
rough drafts for poems or
stories, letters to close friends.

Third : Fast Writing; this is for
rapid notes to yourself, lists
for shopping, telephone
messages, your own personal
thoughts etc.

Printed in Hong Kong by Wing King Tong Co. Lt